Boating and Boats

Boating and Boats

Jill Sutcliffe

London, Henley and Boston
Routledge & Kegan Paul

First published in 1976
by Routledge & Kegan Paul Ltd
39 Store Street, London WC1E 7DD,
Broadway House, Reading Road,
Henley-on-Thames RG9 1EN and
9 Park Street, Boston, Mass. 02108, USA
ISBN 0 7100 8356 4
Filmset and printed in Great Britain by
BAS Printers Limited, Wallop, Hampshire

Frontispiece : *The 40 ft British sloop* 'Cervantes IV' *leads out of Sydney harbour
at the start of a Sydney to Hobart ocean race.*

Contents

'. . . all the business of life is to endeavour to find out what you don't know by what you do'

John Whiting *Marching Song*

Editor's preface

Nobody in Britain lives far from water and, with increasing leisure, more and more people nowadays are becoming interested in boats. There are so many different kinds of boats and so much to do on them that it is no wonder that boating is now one of the most popular of all sports.

Whether you know a lot about boats or very little, this book will help you to find out many things which you may previously have taken for granted or not really thought about. The author tells us about the structure and design of various boats and about their equipment; their many different purposes and the rules and regulations which have to be made and kept if travel on the water is to be at all safe.

An interest in boats can take you far afield, in your mind's eye, if not in real life, for small boats cross the oceans in races, or just as part of man's challenge to the sea. You can go back into history to find boats playing a big part in human activities and progress, you can look for mention of boats in art and literature, or you can find out about modern technological advances such as the hovercraft and hydrofoil.

M.H.

Finding out about boats

Deciding what to include

Safety first

Presenting your project

Boats and a sense of adventure go together. You have only to think of sailing single-handed round the world in a yacht, or racing across the Channel in a motor boat, to understand the excitement of testing your skill against the sea and the weather.

Not all adventure happens at sea, however. It can be found among the many small boats of different kinds in use on rivers, lakes, canals and reservoirs, and even on a boating lake in your local park.

Have you thought of the different uses to which boats are put? Some are needed for safety, some are used for work, and some are just for fun. For example, there are life-boats, ferry boats, and racing dinghies. You will be able to think of many more.

Boat design has a long history. You could try to find out about boats in other countries as well as in Britain. Some, such as the gondola from Venice, have interesting shapes. Others are made from local materials, such as the palm-frond Sha-sha from Arabia. There are also out-riggers and dugouts from islands in the Pacific and from Africa, which you could compare.

You may prefer to make a special feature of modern boats. These could include sailing boats or motor boats. There are several magazines on boating which will give you an idea of current developments. The Boat Show at Earl's Court in London, which takes place in January each year, would give you plenty of material if you could manage a visit.

If you are good at making things, you will want to consider making model boats. See if you can find out how to put a boat

Cruising in style at Horning on the River Bure, Norfolk. Boats like this, with up to seven or eight berths, cooker, refrigerator, shower and w.c., can be hired for holidays.

inside a bottle. You may enjoy making specimens of the knots and splices which boatmen use. If you do this in fairly thick smooth string you can mount the examples on cardboard and label them, describing their uses.

You may decide to make a special study of the Royal National Life-boat Institution and its work. Or you could find out the story of Grace Darling and her father, who made a spectacular rescue of people from a shipwreck off the Farne Islands in 1838. There is a museum at Bamburgh in Northumberland which contains the boat they used.

If you are interested in sport there are many boat races you could watch. You could find out their history, the record winning times and so on. For example, have you heard of Doggett's Coat and Badge? There are the Henley Regatta, Cowes Week, and the Oxford and Cambridge Boat Race, or perhaps you can find a local rowing, sailing, motor boat or canoe club and see if they have their own competitions which you could watch and describe.

Boats appear in stories, poems, songs and pictures. You could look for these in your local library and in museums and art galleries. You will almost certainly be able to watch artists at work around small harbours in the summer months. You could join in with your own sketch book or paints.

Boating people use all kinds of special words such as starboard, tack, and luff. You could make a list of these, with their meanings. Listen to people talking, too. It is surprising how many nautical expressions are used every day. 'To be in the same boat', 'keeping on an even keel', 'putting your oar in', are three to start your collection. What do they mean?

If you can swim (no one should go boating without being able to) perhaps you can find a teacher or youth club leader who will show you how to row, punt, canoe or sail. You could then describe how it is done from first-hand experience. There are many boat clubs, inland as well as at the seaside. If you explain your project to the Club's Secretary he might be prepared to help you. (It is helpful to enclose a stamped envelope, addressed to yourself, for someone to reply if you write asking questions.)

If you plan to go boating, even on your local park lake, it is important to find out first about the safety rules, the 'do's and don'ts' of being on the water. You should not try boating alone until you have had plenty of practice. Certainly if you venture

Launching the Appledore, Devon, life-boat in the late nineteenth century, using horses. It had a narrow beam and heavy keel for stability. Can you see the 'tipping plates' on the outer edge of the large carriage wheel? These prevented the carriage from sinking into the sand. The plates were the forerunners of caterpillar tracks.

The 12·8 m (42 ft) Japanese sloop 'Vago II' using a spinnaker sail.

out on a river, lake or the sea, you should always wear a life-jacket, know something about navigation and weather lore, and find out about local currents and tides. Suitable clothing is also important, so ask an expert what to wear. Boating is fun, but water is dangerous and must always be treated with respect.

A British Waterways Board waterbus running between London Zoo and Little Venice on the Regent's Canal. Notice the life-belts on the roof. This craft can just turn in the width of the canal.

When you have decided what form your study is to take, it is a good idea to carry a notebook with you, to jot down items as you see or hear them. Sketches will be very useful, especially to illustrate technical details. If you have a camera you can liven up your work with suitable photographs.

If you write to anyone for information, think out first exactly what you want to know and ask precise questions. For example, questions about engine sizes or maximum speed can be answered quickly but a vague question such as 'please tell me about motor boats' will not be popular with a busy person.

When you write, give yourself plenty of space. Good margins help to make the pages look neat. If possible use loose sheets of paper and keep them in a folder so that you can add a page

The British Rail cross-Channel hovercraft, 'The Princess Margaret', showing clearly the neoprene skirt, the anchors, radar and four propellers.

if you find some new information, or rearrange the pages if you change your mind about the best order.

Remember to write clear labels or captions for all models and pictures. Other people may not know as much about boats as you do, so you will want to explain everything very clearly for them.

Boat design, equipment and terminology

2

How boats began

The modern boat and its equipment

Boating words

What do you think early man did when he set out to explore the land beyond his immediate surroundings and found his way barred by a deep river or a vast lake? Observing that wood floats in water, he probably set about collecting several stout logs, using his primitive axes. He bound the wood together with whatever he could find, such as reeds twisted or plaited together, or thin, supple lower branches from such trees as the willow, which would be growing by the water. He then stood on this platform or raft in the water and was able to float on it. He also experimented with tree trunks to make a dugout. This boat did not look like the sleek modern canoe. It kept the shape of the tree trunk, with the inside hollowed out roughly.

Movement and control
Early man also had to think about how to move and control his raft or canoe. On the fairly still water of a lake he would have to work hard to move along, using a straight branch as a pole or paddle. On a river, the current would carry him along. His problem then would be to guide the craft clear of rocks or floating branches which might break it up and throw him into the water.

The current would normally take him downstream towards the sea, but if our primitive man were near the mouth of a tidal river, such as the Thames, the incoming tide would at certain times carry him upstream instead, towards the source of the river. Of course it would be very hard work indeed to go against the current with such a primitive kind of boat.

Australian aborigines carved and burnt this canoe from a tree trunk. The plain, at Humpty Doo, south-east of Darwin, is under water during the monsoon season.

A canoe from Sri Lanka.

Have a look at your own nearest river and see how quickly the current carries floating débris along. Can you imagine a primitive raft or canoe on your river? How far would it have been able to go? Would it have met any particular obstacles or dangers?

Improvements in design

When men discovered how design can improve performance in the water, they began to shape their boats. For example, the front end of the canoe (the bow or stem) was made pointed. Can you work out why this was an improvement? The rear end (the stern) was kept square because this helped the balance of

The Fijian proa has a main hull and an 'outrigger' hull (left). Men move about on the joining struts to keep the craft balanced.

the tree-trunk boat and made more space for the man and his belongings. The same reasons — balance and convenience — led to flattening out the bottom of the tree trunk and shaping the sides so that the canoe rested more evenly on the water without rolling over. You will understand more easily how a boat balances on the water if you know how to float yourself. Think how evenly you have to lie in the water and how the slightest lack of balance tips you over. From these early beginnings the modern small boat developed.

You will be able to see old boats and how their design gradually became less clumsy if you can visit the National Maritime Museum at Greenwich. Other museums, especially those in seaside or riverside cities and towns, often have models or actual

Two jalibots from Bahrain. A type of Arab dhow used for fishing. The name probably comes from 'jolly boat', the tender which took crews ashore from bigger ships.

The Queen's Shallop. The original was built in 1698 as State Barge for Queen Mary, consort of William of Orange. This replica is shown at the opening of the Exeter Maritime Museum by Sir Alec Rose.

examples of boats. Look also at pictures in your nearest art gallery and note the dates of paintings and drawings showing boats. Compare the heavy woods, sails and ropes with the lightweight materials used today.

Modern boats and words connected with them

Look first at traditionally made wooden boats. The basis of a boat is its keel. This may be deep or shallow, depending on the purpose of the boat. You may have heard someone say 'the keel has been laid', meaning the foundation has been put down for building a new boat. The keel runs from stem to stern, acting as a backbone and helping the boat to balance. Obviously, like a human backbone, it must be strong. At the front it ends in an upright stem-post, and at the back in a stern-post.

As the boat has a backbone, it also has ribs or timbers (hence the expression 'shiver my timbers', meaning you are in such a difficult situation that the timbers of your boat are shaking). The Victorian skiff on page 12 shows the different parts of a boat's structure. As its name suggests, the gunwale (pronounced gunn'l) which forms the top edge would have supported guns in a big ship, but in a rowing boat it holds the oars. These fit either into metal crutches or into holes made for them (not shown here) called rowlocks (pronounced rollocks). The seats are called thwarts, because they lie athwart, or across, the boat.

The sides of the boat, covering the framework of ribs, are made of wooden planks. If the planks overlap, the boat is known as clinker-built. If the planks fit flush (that is, meet edge to edge) the boat is carvel-built.

If your local park has a boating lake, or if you live near a river or harbour where there are small boats, examine a wooden rowing boat and identify the different parts. You will not be able to see the keel because this will be underneath the planks where the oarsmen put their feet. To see this, look for a boat which is out of the water.

If you can find different shapes and sizes of rowing boat, decide which you would choose for a beginner to learn to row.

Do you think a wide, short boat is less likely or more likely to capsize (turn over) than a long, narrow boat? Which kind of boat would an experienced oarsman prefer?

Now look around at newer rowing boats. Nowadays these are often made of glass-fibre, which means that they are moulded all in one piece, without the elaborate construction of wooden boats. See how many advantages you can think of that glass-fibre has over wood.

Victorian skiff made of mahogany. The rudder and steering ropes are lying on the passenger seat. Note the wrought iron back.

Avon S100 Sportboat. This inflatable craft has an outboard engine but notice the rowlocks for oars.

Another kind of modern rowing boat is the inflatable rubber boat. Compare all three kinds of boat for cost, ease of handling, and safety.

Sailing boats
The smallest sailing boat you are likely to see is a dinghy. The dinghy can sail on lakes, rivers or reservoirs (when boating is allowed there) because it does not need very deep water. It has what is called a shallow draught. This means that because the boat is wide and has only a small keel its weight is spread over a wide surface of water so that most of the structure stays above water. Larger boats which have steeper sides, are heavier, and have a deep keel to keep the boat balanced; they have a deeper draught and need deeper water.

Sailing equipment
Many people think they know what a yacht looks like. You can probably draw from memory a boat with a mast and sails. Try it and then find out how accurate you have been.

Do you know how the mast stays upright? How are the sails attached to it? What shape are they?

Look at pictures of sailing boats and see if you can identify different classes of boat by their distinctive sails, the height and shape of mast, length and other details. Then you may find it useful to visit a sailing club or a marina, which is a place

Dinghy club sailing on the Welsh Harp, a BWB reservoir in north London. The boats are GP14s ('General Purpose 14 ft'), designed by Jack Holt for 'Yachting World' magazine. The bell you can see on the sail shows the class, named after the main builder of this boat, Bell Woodworking Co. of Leicester.

where small boats can moor. See if you can recognise the sails and parts of boats when they are actually in use.

Ropes

Sails are hoisted and lowered by ropes called halyards. Ropes which control the sails once they are hoisted are called sheets. All these ropes are known as running rigging. Can you work out why? Find out which ropes are the mainsheet, main halyard, jib halyard and hoist, and what each one is used for.

Wires

If you think of a yacht in full sail in a good wind you will realise how strong the mast has to be to support the sails. To help it stay up it is usually strengthened by wires attaching it to the boat. These are known as standing rigging because they are fixed in position. See if you can find out which part of the mast the various wires are attached to, where they are fitted to the boat itself, and what they are called. When you have found out all these details you will be able to draw a really accurate picture of a sailing boat.

The rudder and the centre-board

Most of the rudder and the centre-board are usually under the water so you may not have seen exactly what they look like. See if you can find a boat out of the water and examine its rudder and the centre-board case. You will notice that the rudder is hinged to the stern and that it is moved about by a handle at the top, called the tiller. What is the effect on the direction of the boat of pushing the tiller to the left or to the right?

'Stormy', a Dutch entry in the 1971 Sydney–Hobart ocean race. Can you identify the sails and rigging of this 15·8 m (52 ft) yawl?

The centre-board acts as a temporary deep keel for a normally shallow-keeled dinghy. A dinghy is launched from shallow water with the centre-board up, and as soon as the boat reaches deep enough water the centre-board is lowered. It helps to balance the boat and keep it on a straight course. The board has to be raised when coming in to shallow water again. Watch people launching boats, to see how it works.

Direction

You may have heard a radio programme called 'The Navy Lark' in which one of the characters steers the boat by saying 'left hand down a bit'. This would, of course, be quite unprofessional! A proper sailor would say port for left and starboard for right and would steer more precisely. You can probably find out for yourself how these terms came to be used. They apply to anything left or right of an imaginary line drawn down the middle of a boat, facing forward towards the bows or stem. If you turn round and face the stern, port and starboard do not change sides with you. Port would then be on *your* right hand side and starboard on *your* left. In other words, although you had changed position the left and right hand sides of the boat would stay the same.

Study the drawing on page 17 and fix the terms in your mind so that you can use them confidently. Draw your own sketch from memory. You will need to explain the terms carefully in your work for the benefit of non-sailors or 'land-lubbers'.

Modern materials

The traditional materials for boat building, mainly wood, canvas and rope, have been used for centuries and sailors know they are reliable. Man enjoys experimenting, however, and cost plays a part, too, so many boats are now being made of glass-fibre. Sails and ropes, too, are usually now made of man-made fibres. What advantages can you think of that man-made materials may have over natural ones? A clue to this is 'maintenance'. Try to visit a boat club at the end of the summer and see what the boat owners have to do to make sure their boats

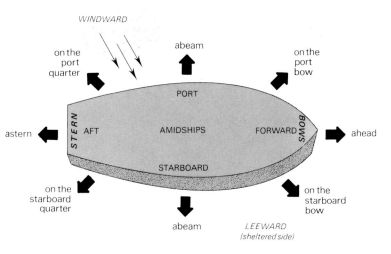

Boating words.

are seaworthy for the next season. You can discover more about this if you can find a boat yard where boats are laid up for the winter, or if you can talk to a fisherman about how he maintains his boat. He probably uses it all the year round, so how does he keep it in good order?

Ropework

A rope is made up of many thin strands of fibre twisted together for strength. To test this, collect as many different kinds of string as you can. Notice what happens when you twist the string anti-clockwise and then clockwise. Do all the strands lie in the same direction? See how two strands are woven or wrapped around each other, and then see how each major strand is made up of many really thin fibres. Even the thinnest string is made up of different strands.

You may also find some cord, such as picture cord, or a lanyard worn with some uniforms, which is braided or plaited for strength or decoration.

Note that some string is coarse and rough to handle, while some is fine and soft. Some is stiff and unbending while some is flexible. This depends on what the string is made of. It may be sisal or hemp, cotton or a synthetic fibre.

All this applies to rope, too, which is made in the same way but

A corner of a chandler's shop. How many items can you identify?

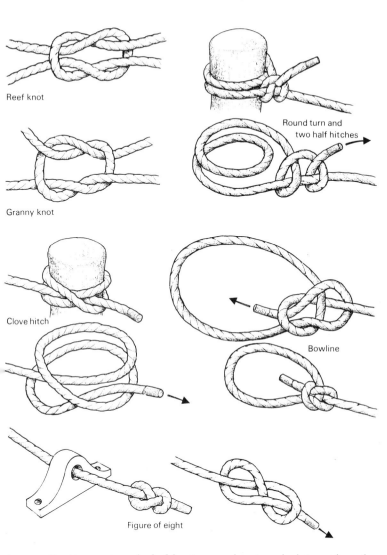

Ropework.

Reef knot

Round turn and
two half hitches

Granny knot

Clove hitch

Bowline

Figure of eight

is usually three-stranded. Most rope is stranded together (or laid up) in a clockwise direction, though there are exceptions.

See if you can find out the best kinds of rope for different uses on a boat. For example, which kind is best for use as a mainsheet? What advantage would 'terylene' have over 'nylon' in running rigging? Why would 'nylon' be good for use as a painter (the mooring rope)? Compare the effect of water on a natural fibre rope and on one of man-made fibre. You may have to visit a ship's chandler or store to ask about this. Or you may find a fisherman willing to 'show you the ropes'. Sailors have to be experts with ropes and knots and they may be pleased to talk to you about ropecraft if you ask when they are not too busy.

When you unravelled your pieces of string did you notice how the ends began to fray almost at once? To stop this happening, all rope in use needs to have its ends whipped or bound up in some way. Try to find someone to show you how to do this.

You should find out why different knots are used at different times. Particularly useful is the reef knot. Why is this better than a 'granny' knot? You will find this out if you try to undo both kinds.

How many boating knots, bends and hitches can you discover? Try to examine them actually in use on a boat. Perhaps you could moor a model boat to a ring or a stake as part of your display, and show other ropes in use, with explanations.

The anchor
The rowing boat on the park pond will not need an anchor but if you took a boat out fishing, for example, you might need one. You probably already know what an anchor looks like. Try to identify its different parts. There is more than one kind of anchor. See if you can find at least two designs and ask questions to discover when each kind is used.

Leisure boats

3

Hand-powered boats

Sail-driven boats

Boats with engines

Model boats

Why do so many people nowadays go boating for fun? Perhaps it is because families can take their boat by car, so that reaching the sea or a convenient inland waterway is no longer the problem it once was. Living in crowded cities may make people want to escape to the peace and fresh air of a boat on the water. The motor boat enthusiast must have other reasons, though, as his craft is noisy. It might be interesting to ask people who go boating why they took up the hobby and see how many different answers they give you.

Canoeing

The modern canoe is possibly the most suitable boat for young people to use. It is light in weight, not too expensive to make or buy, and it can be used on small rivers.

Its lightness, however, does make it unstable in the water and liable to roll over, so you need to have a good sense of balance. The shape of the canoe – long, narrow and with hardly any keel – makes it a very fast boat which can twist and turn through rapids, but for the same reasons it takes skill to control.

The canoe is propelled by a paddle, with either a single or a double blade. Look out on rivers for canoeists using both types of paddle and ask questions to find out which is best for different kinds of canoe and different purposes.

Most canoes you will see are kayaks, descended from the

A Tyne Senior kayak.

Eskimo canoe. There are several different designs for different purposes, such as touring, racing and 'white water' slalom racing. Slalom involves steering the boat through rough water round poles suspended upright over the water. It is similar to ski slalom races you may have seen on television or on winter sports' holidays.

See if you can find rigid and folding canoes, and look to see if they have a hard or soft 'skin'. In other words, are they made with a wooden frame over which waterproofed canvas has been stretched, or is the hull solid, as in a glass-fibre boat? Why do you think some canoes are made to fold up? Ask someone to show you how they are put together and taken apart.

Because the kayak capsizes easily it is important to know how to right it. A technique called 'the roll' has been borrowed from the Eskimo, who must stay in his boat even if it capsizes, because he would not survive otherwise in the icy water. The canoeist rolls under the water with the canoe, staying in the cockpit, and uses his paddle to roll the boat upright again on the other side. Of course this has to be learnt under expert guidance and not by experimenting on your own.

The second major type of canoe is known as the Canadian, which developed from the American Indian canoe. Canadians are rigid canoes and mostly have a hard skin. Canadian touring canoes are not completely closed-in like kayaks and have more space for stowing kit. Because they are roomy they are often crewed by more than one person, using single-bladed paddles. The Canadian racing canoe differs from the racing kayak in several ways. See if you can discover the differences.

A Canadian type (Red Indian) canoe shown on an American stamp. Who was Marquette?

If you want to try canoeing it is essential to be able to swim. This sport is definitely not for non-swimmers. Join a canoe club and with some practice you should be able to pass the British Canoe Union Proficiency Test. Then you can safely explore quite long stretches of your local river, go in for races or try your hand at slalom.

It is easy to see why the canoeist faces the direction in which he is travelling: it would not be safe to negotiate rapids in a fast-moving boat unless you could see where you were going.

Punting

Another boat in which the person propelling it faces forward is the punt. By contrast to the canoe, though, the punt is a very slow boat, so can you think why you have to face forward in this case? The reason is the long pole which you put into the water until it touches the river bed and then lean on to lever your way along. This is not as easy as it sounds because if you do not stop leaning on the pole at the right moment you may find the boat has moved forward and left you and the pole behind. You will probably be able to find books with amusing pictures of this happening, or if you can find people punting you may see it actually happen to one of them. Have your camera ready!

Because a punt is a flat, shallow boat it can only be used on calm water. It also needs a fairly level river bed beneath it to take the pole. Consequently you will not see it in many places. The river Cam at Cambridge is one well-known punting place, and you should be able to find punts at various points along the Thames.

Punting was especially popular earlier this century because it is a slow and elegant pastime suitable for well-dressed young ladies and gentlemen. The men wore straw hats called 'boaters', striped blazers and white flannel trousers, and the women sat in the punts wearing pretty dresses and hats and using a parasol to shade themselves from the sun.

Rowing boats

One obvious difference between the rowing boat and the canoe or punt is that in a rowing boat the oarsman travels backwards. See how many other differences you can think of between these boats. How much are these differences due to the design of the boat, to the kind of water on which it is used, or to its purpose?

Your first acquaintance with a rowing boat may well be on the boating lake in a park or in a boat hired for an hour on a quiet stretch of river. You can quickly learn the likely problems and the techniques of rowing by standing on the bank and watching other people in their boats.

How easy is it to get into or out of a boat? What happens when the oarsman uses one oar instead of two? If there is a passenger look and see what he or she does to help the oarsman. If there is no passenger what must the oarsman remember to do?

Relaxing on the river. Compare the rowlocks with the Victorian skiff's. Can you see how the girl is steering?

If your boat is heavy you may find it easier to sit with a friend beside you and each of you take one oar. Even this can create problems. Try it and see what happens. Remember to be very careful how you move about in the boat. Only one person should move at a time or you will risk capsizing. Never experiment in deep water.

Rowing for fun calls for less skill than rowing for racing. Racing boats are much lighter in weight than the ordinary rowing boat. They are narrower and often longer. They have sliding seats to give the oarsman more power to his stroke. There are races for

The winning home-made boat in a charity race on the Severn. It was made from two US Air Force wing drop tanks obtained from an army surplus dealer. The crew was from the Central Electricity Generating Board's power station at Ironbridge.

the single oarsman, but usually racing is done by a crew of two, four or eight. The larger crews usually carry a coxswain (pronounced cox'n), who is in charge of the boat, gives the orders and steers. The first oarsman is called stroke, and the others take their time from him, rather like players in an orchestra following their leader.

What else do you notice about oars and oarsmen in a racing boat that is different from what you expect to see in a pleasure boat?

Sailing boats

A small boat under sail demands less effort than a hand-powered boat, but you have to learn how to handle sails and to understand the wind and weather. Sailing will almost certainly take you on to larger and deeper stretches of water than a hand-powered boat will, so it is sensible to wear a life-jacket. The best and safest way to find out about sailing is to take lessons from a sailing school, to join a club, or find an experienced boat-owner who will take you along as crew and show you what to do.

If you visit a club there are some sailing techniques and terms to ask about and to see demonstrated if possible. What special ourpose has the burgee or little flag at the top of the mast? Find out what tacking is and how you do it. What does sailing close o the wind mean? You may have heard this expression used in everyday speech. What does it mean then? Ask what might happen if you were to gybe accidentally. If you were sailing single-handed you would need to 'heave-to' to reef sails. What would this involve? If you need to drop anchor it is not sufficient just to throw the anchor overboard. What would you have to remember?

Mooring a sailing boat is quite an art if you are not going to collide with another boat or scratch your paintwork. How you do it depends on the direction of the wind and the tide, if there is one. Watch people manoeuvring their boats up to a landing stage or a buoy and see if you can spot the experts and the beginners. Then try to find an expert to tell you how it should be done. If a sailing boat has to be moored to a buoy in deep water, how does the crew come ashore? It is interesting to watch moored boats when the tide changes and to see what happens to them.

Besides dinghies you may see cabin cruisers carrying sails. These are larger boats with room for sleeping, cooking, etc. People often hire these for a cruising holiday, on the Norfolk Broads, for example.

Live-aboard holiday yacht on the Norfolk Broads. Making adjustments to the boom.

You may also see a type of boat called a catamaran. This has two identical hulls joined together across the deck and with supporting struts between the hulls. The water flows between the two hulls. A 'cat', as it is known for short, carries the same rig as a single-hulled boat. People have different views about this craft. Those in favour of it say it is fast and strong. Those against it say it is dangerous if it capsizes. Obviously it would be very heavy to right again. The trimaran is similar in design, but with three hulls. The same arguments apply to this boat. See if you can talk to people who have sailed in a cat or a tri and hear both points of view.

For racing purposes sailing boats are divided into classes, so that boats of the same size and power can race against each other. There are also handicap races for boats of mixed classes.

Trimarans in harbour at Townsville, Queensland, Australia.

Letters, numbers or symbols displayed on the sails tell you the class of a boat. For example F is for Firefly, N for National, and

C for Cadet. Dinghies range from 2·3 m (7 ft 6 ins) long up to almost 6 m (20 ft) in length. Take your notebook and do some class-spotting. A copy of the rules of the International Yacht Racing Union can be obtained from the Royal Yachting Association.

Motor boats

You may be able to 'drive' a fairly sedate motor boat in a seaside boating pool. If this gives you a taste for more speed you should try out motor boats on larger stretches of water.

Watch a fast boat in action and note what happens. You will see that it does not travel through the water in quite the same way as boats that are not power driven. The bows lift right out of the water and at a certain speed the boat seems almost to take off into the air. See what you can find out about why this happens. You might also like to find out how important the size of the engine is in relation to the weight of the boat, what fuel is used and how much you need for an afternoon's fun. A motor boat churns up the water and makes waves as it rushes along. It is inconsiderate to take a motor boat at speed through a crowd of other small boats. One way of having fun with a motor boat is to use it for water-skiing. The water needs to be calm and you have to watch out for the safety of other boats and skiers. See what you can find out about this sport and how to handle a boat which is towing a skier.

You might enjoy power boat racing. Serious racing is organised at an international level by the UIM (Union Internationale Moto-nautique) in Belgium. Each country affiliated to the UIM has its own national racing authority.

Powerful boats in Classes I and II race as far as 322 km (200 miles). The smaller Class III boats cover up to 161 km (100 miles). See what you can find out about the Paris six-hour race, the Cowes to Torquay and back, and the Cross-Channel race. For example, find out when they are held, what classes of boat compete, what the prizes are and how many competitors usually enter. You might also like to discover how long the winner takes and what speed the winning boat achieves.

*Skin-diving party
using an Avon S650
Sportboat.*

You might enjoy tracing the history of the British International Trophy races which started in 1903 when Sir Alfred Harmsworth offered a cup for power boat racing. Linked with this is the international struggle to win and hold the world water speed record. Do you know who holds this now and what the speed is? The *Guinness Book of Records* will tell you.

Hovercraft

A more recent development is the use of one-, two- or four-seater hovercraft for cruising and racing. The Hover Club of Great Britain arranges races every year. These are held in such places as the Trossachs in Scotland and the Cotswold Water Park near Cirencester. The Club also organises an annual Schools National Hovercraft Competition for school-built hovercraft, on behalf of the sponsors, British Petroleum and the *Daily Express*. School hovercraft have reached about 48 kph (about 30 mph).

Narrow boats

In the summer you may see people holiday-making along a stretch of canal in narrow boats. These are so called because their maximum beam, or width, is 2·1 m (7 ft), otherwise they could not navigate narrow canals. The original narrow boats that worked the canals were usually 21 m (70 ft) long, but for holidaymakers, who are not necessarily expert boatmen, boats about 9–10 m (around 30 ft) long are used. They are steered either from a tiller positioned aft or from a central cockpit, and the engine uses either petrol or diesel oil. Even in the confined space below deck, such a boat will contain berths for four people, a table, calor gas cooker, refrigerator, and toilet facilities. Imagine the planning that goes into fitting all this in, and how tidy the people on board have to be!

You might like to find out how these boats negotiate the locks on the canals, how far they can travel in a day, what hazards they are likely to meet, and how they turn round to come back at the end of the holiday.

Because trains and lorries are quicker than canal boats for carrying goods, the number of working boats on the canals gradually decreased. (They may become more popular again now that fuel is more expensive.) With fewer boats using them,

Waiting for the water level to fall in Buckby top lock Northants so that the narrow boat can go under the road bridge beyond the lock.

many of the smaller canals were not kept in good repair. They became choked with weeds, the banks crumbled, and people threw rubbish into them. Now that there is a growing interest in boating for fun these canals are being cleaned, repaired and re-opened. Much of the credit for this is due to the British Waterways Board, and to the Inland Waterways Association which campaigns on behalf of people interested in canals. Societies have been formed by people interested in their local canals. One example is the Staffordshire & Worcestershire Canal Society, which was formed in 1959 to save its canal for boating, canoeing, fishing, and so on. Many of these societies do voluntary restoration work, especially in the winter months. You might find it interesting to volunteer to help. You could describe how the canal looks before the particular job starts and how it looks afterwards, with pictures if possible, and you could record what work you did yourself.

Model boats

If you live inland and have no boats nearby, you can still take an interest in them through boat-modelling. This can be an

Sailing model boats in a boating pond near the sea-front at Aldeburgh, Suffolk.

absorbing hobby. Some people take many months to reconstruct in great detail, and exactly to scale, a model of a particular boat in which they are interested. Museums often have models of boats of all kinds which you can study.

If you want a boat which you can sail on the local pond you can make one which is less detailed but more robust: a boat to use and not just to look at. You can buy kits from modelling or toy shops to make many different types of boat.

If you are really ambitious you can fit your model with equipment to make it radio controlled, so that it will change direction at your command. You may be able to join a model boat club and enter your model for races.

4   Working boats

Fishing boats

Police, and Customs and Excise boats

Life-boats

Hovercraft and hydrofoils

To find working boats you may need to look in a different part of a harbour or river from where you see the leisure craft.

Fishing boats

It is convenient to keep boats which smell strongly of fish well away from the Sunday afternoon boating family, and the fisherman, too, does not want to find a leisure boat in the way as he hurries to catch a particular tide. Fishing boats will need deeper water and bigger landing stages than most leisure boats use.

Inshore fishermen can be seen at many places around the coast. They may go out to attend to lobster pots, or to let out nets or lines. They may fish for a living or they may hire out their boats to sea anglers. If you visit Cornwall ask the boatmen there about shark fishing. Looe is one centre for this activity. The boats used are about 11 m (36 ft) long, with two engines for safety, because they go out into the Atlantic for a distance of 22–32 km (14–20 miles) and they have to contend with big seas as well as with the sharks.

Look at the equipment the inshore fisherman uses. He will have boxes or baskets for the fish. There will be piles of nets. Ask him how far out to sea he goes compared with the deep-sea fishermen, what kinds of fish he catches, how he knows where the fish are likely to be, and what he does with them when he has caught them.

Sea-going fishing boat moored at Burnham-on-Crouch, Essex. How much can you find out about the equipment of a boat like this?

Police boats

In ports and harbours around the coast and on large rivers, police officers patrol. They are there to prevent or deal with crime, especially theft from ships' cargoes and warehouses, to detect the movement of 'wanted' persons in or out of the country, and to investigate drowning and other accidents.

The 'Thames' Division of the Metropolitan Police, whose headquarters are at Wapping and whose 'beat' extends for about 85 km (54 miles) from Staines Bridge in Middlesex to Dartford Creek in Kent on the south shore and to Havering Borough boundary on the north shore, use 9 m (30 ft) long duty boats with glass-fibre hulls and cabins. These boats are powered by a single 74·6 kW (100 hp) diesel engine. If you should spot a police launch with a wooden cabin you will have made a 'find' because there are only three in the Division. They are used by senior officers for supervisory and ceremonial duties. The flag which flies from the stern is a Blue Ensign defaced with the badge of the Metropolitan Police. ('Defaced' here is a heraldic word meaning that the badge is added to the normal Blue Ensign. It does not have the usual meaning of 'damaged'.) The unique privilege of using this flag was granted by Admiralty Warrant in 1952.

The duty boats have a crew of three. They carry drags for recovering objects under the water, lifebuoys, and an automatic machine for artificial respiration in case someone they rescue from the water is unconscious and needs help to restore their breathing.

The Strathclyde Police River Patrol, based on Glasgow, has a large area to cover. It extends from the Clyde in Glasgow itself to approximately the northern tip of Arran. This takes in Holy Loch and Loch Fyne, and is about 1150 square kilometres (450 square miles).

The River Patrol began in Glasgow in 1890 with a rowing boat bought for the police for £16. This proved inadequate, so a motor launch was borrowed from the Sewage Department until money was found for the police to have their own launch. Their latest launch 'Semper Vigilo II' (Latin for 'Always Vigilant'), came into service in 1971. It was built locally for £32,000.

Apart from normal police duties the River Patrol attends all launchings of ships on the Clyde, escorts oil rigs, and deals with oil pollution. It also works closely with the Underwater Search Unit.

H.M. Customs and Excise boats

H.M. Customs and Excise officers patrol coastal waters, ports and harbours to make sure boats are not being used for smuggling. They use launches to board and rummage ships which arrive from foreign ports. Their boats range from small dinghies with outboard motors to Revenue Cutters large enough to go to sea. You can recognise a Customs boat by its Blue Ensign flag with a portcullis design added to it.

Hovercraft and hydrofoils

The hovercraft was invented by Sir Christopher Cockerell and was pioneered in Britain in the 1950s. Air is blown by a fan to form a 'cushion' which is contained inside a 'skirt' so that the boat literally floats on air, just above the surface of the water. The tough, flexible skirt helps the craft to negotiate waves

Big hovercraft are powered by gas turbines and small ones by petrol or diesel engines.

You can see commercial hovercraft working between Ryde on the Isle of Wight and Southsea, between Southampton and Cowes, across the Channel between Dover, Calais and Boulogne, and between Pegwell Bay, near Ramsgate, and Calais. You could draw a map of the Channel and South Coast showing these routes. You can find out from travel agents' leaflets how long the crossings take.

Customs officers boarding a ship from their motor launch. How many details can you write down about their boat?

The cross-Channel SR.N4 Mountbatten class hovercraft carry up to 254 passengers and 30 cars at a maximum speed of about 60 knots. Their four Proteus gas turbine engines are each of 2,536 kW (3,400 hp). The SR.N6 Winchester class craft on the Cowes–Southampton and Ryde–Southsea routes reach 50 knots using one Gnome 671 kW (900 hp) engine. These craft

*British Rail hovercraft
on the Cowes–
Southampton run.*

carry 56 passengers. The number and power of the engines used depend on the design and weight of the craft, its load, and the kind of weather conditions it is likely to meet.

Small hovercraft carrying as few as one or two people are being used in different parts of the world for various purposes. For example, medical missionaries use them on Lake Chad in Central Africa, and in Canada hovercraft are used to keep water free from ice on the Great Lakes. Hovercraft also have military uses as patrol vessels and landing craft. Explorers are using hovercraft, too, because they can travel over rapids where ordinary boats would capsize or break up.

Like the hovercraft, the hydrofoil is moved by lifting the hull of the boat above the water. This is done by means of foils or struts underneath the hull. These act like aircraft wings by creating lift as they move forward in the water.

Ferry boats
A ferry takes people across a river, or sometimes from one side of a large harbour to another, so that they do not have to make a long detour to reach the other side. The boat may be a small open boat for a few passengers or it may be a substantial engine-driven craft. An example of the first kind can be seen at King's Lynn in Norfolk and of the second kind at Birkenhead in Cheshire. Look on an Ordnance Survey map or a detailed motoring map and see how many ferries are marked in your area.

You could draw your own ferry map. Imagine you are on a journey along the coast and compare the distance travelled taking the ferries and taking the nearest inland road.

If you can visit a ferry you will see that the larger ones usually work in pairs, one from each bank, to avoid keeping people waiting. You may find it interesting to see exactly how long it takes to load, cross the water and unload. Do both boats cross in exactly the same time, or does the current affect the time each takes?

Life-boats

There are two main kinds of life-boat: (1) those carried by ships to enable passengers and crew to escape in an emergency and (2) boats launched from the shore by the Royal National Life-boat Institution (RNLI) to rescue people from the sea. Ships' life-boats can also include life-rafts and inflatable rubber

Cleaning a life-boat and its davit on the P & O liner 'Arcadia'. Notice the life-boat number and the series of pulleys and hawsers that will let the boat down into the sea.

boats, but the boats you will think of immediately are the white-painted rowing boats slung along the decks of a passenger ship. If you travel on a ship, examine how the life-boats are held in position and the machinery for lowering them into the water.

See if you can find a notice on the ship explaining the life-boat drill. You could ask at the Purser's office if one of the crew might spare a few minutes to tell you how long it takes to launch a life-boat, how many people each one carries and how often the boats are lowered for practice.

How many RNLI life-boat stations are there in the British Isles? Draw a map of the coast nearest your home, mark on it the local life-boat stations and see how much you can find out about them.

The older classes of life-boat are the Barnett, 15·8 m (52 ft) working mainly from harbours; the Watson, 14·3–14·6 m (47–8 ft), usually launched from life-boat houses; the 12·8 m (42 ft) Watson, often launched down an open slipway on a steep beach; and the 10·8 m (35 ft 6 ins) and 11·3 m (37 ft) Oakley, mainly taken by tractor across a flat beach. Some of these are being replaced by more modern designs such as the 15·8 m (52 ft) Arun, 15·2 m (50 ft) Thames, 14·8 (48 ft 6 ins)

A tractor pushing the Bridlington (11·3 m) 37 ft Oakley life-boat out to sea.

Solent and 13·4 m (44 ft) Waveney classes. The Waveney is built to a design used by the US Coast Guard.

Modern life-boats have twin diesel engines and are usually equipped with radio, echo sounder and radar. In 1975 they cost about £150,000 each, and costs are still increasing. Because the RNLI is a voluntary organisation the money is raised from the public by coffee mornings, flag days, bequests in people's wills, and membership of 'Shoreline' (by making an annual subscription).

The crews are volunteers who work at other jobs when they are not called out to try to save lives at sea. Some people think life-boatmen should be paid employees but others (including the RNLI itself) prefer volunteers. Discuss it with your friends and see what reasons you can think of on both sides.

At seaside resorts you may see Inshore Life-boats (ILBs). These were introduced in 1963 and have already saved over 5,100 lives, mainly in the summer rescuing swimmers, and people from leisure boats. The standard craft are 4·9 m (16 ft) and are inflatable, being made of Neoprene nylon fabric. They have an outboard 29·8 kW (40 hp) engine and a crew of two, and can carry up to ten people. A new class, the Atlantic 6·4 m (21 ft), is semi-inflatable, having a rigid hull. This has twin 37·3 kW (50 hp) engines and can reach almost 30 knots.

Most life-boat stations welcome visitors and you might be lucky enough to see a practice launching. The local RNLI Secretary would be able to tell you when a practice is due.

Canal boats

You may still be able to find a full-length working narrow boat on one of the canals in the Birmingham or Wolverhampton area but there are not many left in Britain now. They are brightly painted, have polished brass fittings and decorative rope work, all of traditional designs. The Waterways Museum at Stoke Bruerne on the Grand Canal near Towcester, Northants, is well worth visiting if you want to know more about these boats.

You will see 'barges' of various kinds on the bigger canals and

Pusher-tug with composite craft carrying up to 500 tons (just over 500 tonnes) of coal to Ferrybridge Power Station on the Aire and Calder Navigation. You can also see older barges, and beyond, a group of 'Tom Puddings' at their moorings.

A collection of working boats, narrow boats and houseboats near Little Venice, London.

rivers. Often these are towed or pushed in a long string by a tug. They carry coal, gravel and other heavy goods. On the Thames these boats are called lighters. On the Aire and Calder Navigation in Yorkshire you may see 'Tom Puddings', box-shaped containers linked together behind a tug.

Other working boats
Keep your eyes open for other kinds of small working boat: houseboats in which people live, moored by a river bank; water buses which run on a regular route on a river or canal; and boats used by British Waterways Board officials for inspecting and maintaining river and canal banks.

5   Boats in history

To America by reed boat?

Kon-Tiki   The Graveney Boat

Coracles

The Second World War

Men have used boats for exploration, trade, war, and flight from danger almost since time began. You might enjoy finding out about the boats of pre-Christian civilisations such as the ancient Egyptians or the Phoenicians, and what part boats played in the lives of people who lived near great rivers such as the Nile, or on the Mediterranean coast.

To America by reed boat?
In the 1960s Thor Heyerdahl, a Norwegian, decided to try out his theory that Egyptians, Phoenicians or some other early Mediterranean people had crossed the Atlantic Ocean in reed boats to take their civilisation to South and Central America, long before Columbus 'discovered' America in AD 1492. He had observed that not only were reed boats known all around the Mediterranean in Egyptian and Phoenician times but that boats of similar design, made of papyrus reeds, were known and used by the inhabitants of Easter Island in the Pacific and the Indians of Lake Titicaca on the borders of Bolivia and Peru in South America.

Heyerdahl wondered if this was a coincidence, or if these people had been taught by visitors from the Mediterranean. The first thing to do was to find out if a papyrus reed boat was capable of floating in the salt water and rough conditions of the Atlantic. Hardly anyone thought it possible. They thought the reeds would sink after a few days.

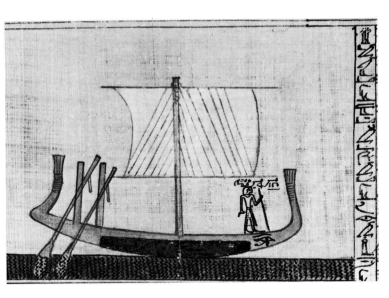

The ancient Egyptians thought the dead sailed boats in the next world.

In spite of people's doubts he went ahead with his idea, building his boat on the sand near the Giza pyramid in Egypt. He copied the design from paintings of reed boats found inside the pyramid tombs of the Egyptian Pharoahs, and he brought skilled reed boat builders to Egypt from Lake Chad in Central Africa.

The papyrus came from the upper Nile. It grows about 2 m (about 6 ft) long and is about 5 cms (about 2 ins) thick at the base. It has a spongy filling, like foam rubber. When these reeds were worked into one another and tied very tightly in big bundles they proved to be amazingly tough. When it was ready the boat, called *Ra*, was taken by land and sea to the ancient Moroccan port of Safi, where it was launched for its long voyage.

You may enjoy finding out more about Heyerdahl's adventure and the theories about who really did discover America first. See if you can find out why he chose his crew from different countries. Look into the details of what food they took with them and the kinds of fish they caught; how long they were at sea and what they found out about how man is polluting the sea with waste materials.

Not long after the first expedition Heyerdahl made a second reed

Sha-sha from Batinha on the Arabian coast. Made mostly from the stems of date palm fronds.

boat, called *Ra II*. This time he used the techniques of Lake Titicaca Indian boat builders. Can you find out why, and what the differences were?

If you look at Heyerdahl's book, *The Ra Expeditions,* you will find colour photographs of reed boats which would help you to make your own model boats or drawings.

Kon-Tiki

Not long after the Second World War — before he sailed in *Ra* — Thor Heyerdahl had a similar adventure with a raft. On that occasion he tested the theory that the fair-skinned sun king Kon-Tiki, who had been driven out of Peru by the Incas, could

Another simple boat, from Lobito Bay, Angola.

have been carried by ocean currents across the Pacific to the Polynesian islands. Heyerdahl built a balsa-wood raft based on traditional American Indian design. With five companions he sailed it from Callao in Peru and they reached Raroia, a Polynesian island, a hundred days later. The islanders instantly recognised the craft as a *pae-pae,* the kind of raft their ancestors had used. You can read about this exciting adventure in *The Kon-Tiki Expedition.*

The Graveney Boat, showing clearly its ribs and timbers.

The Graveney Boat

There is a growing interest in boating archaeology in Britain. Remains of boats are sometimes uncovered when builders move into river- or sea-side sites with their bulldozers. The Graveney Boat was found in the Graveney Marshes near Whitstable in 1970. Dating from the ninth century AD it had been preserved by the 2·4 m (8 ft) of clay which had covered it. It was carefully dug out and is now in the care of the National Maritime Museum.

Coracles

These ancient boats were so practical that they are still made and used today. The coracle is usually round or oval, about 1·2–1·5 m (4–5 ft) across, but some are oblong in shape. Originally the framework of laths was covered with animal skins, but today unbleached calico is stretched tightly over it and then treated with tar and pitch. The coracle is propelled by one paddle, leaving the boatman's other hand free for fishing.

In Britain we usually think of the coracle as a Welsh boat, but they were also used in England, on the river Severn for instance. A Shrewsbury coracle dating from about 1936 can be seen in Rowley's House Museum there.

Net fishing was officially stopped on the Severn in the late 1920s to conserve the stock of fish, and the coracle has almost died out there. One coracle-maker remains in Ironbridge, Shropshire, making coracles and models of them for use on privately owned water, for museums, and for export to Australia, Germany, Israel, New Zealand and elsewhere.

The Irish, too, have a type of coracle, known as a curragh or currach. Tradition has it that St Patrick may have arrived in Ireland in one of these.

See if you can find pictures, or examples in museums, of Welsh, Irish and English coracles. Compare them for size and shape and find out on which rivers they were used. In Wales net fishing has not yet completely died out because sons were allowed to inherit their fathers' fishing permits, so you may be lucky enough to see a coracle still in use there.

The late Tommy Rogers, from a well-known coracle-making family at Iron-bridge, with his coracle. Note the framework, carrying strap and spade-like paddle.

Eustace Rogers, grandson of Tommy Rogers, and the only coracle-maker now left at Ironbridge, showing a modern coracle in action.

The Second World War

During the Second World War small boats were used in many dramatic ways. One occasion which vitally affected the survival of Britain was the evacuation of the British Expeditionary Force and part of the French army from Dunkirk in the early summer of 1940.

A fleet of assorted small boats crossed and re-crossed the Channel to help rescue 338,226 men. Many boats were sunk or damaged by mines, torpedoes and aerial attack.

The boats included many privately owned motor yachts from boat clubs, from Great Yarmouth on the East Coast to Poole in Dorset. It was a great achievement for these craft even to cross the Channel. Many had only a small converted car engine, not a marine engine designed for going to sea. Much skill and courage was shown by the crews, many of whom had little or no sleep for a week. Can you imagine how hard they worked to rescue so many soldiers? If you think of the number of people in an average crowd at a First Division football match and multiply that by ten, you can picture the size of the problem.

There were many other daring wartime adventures involving small boats. See what you can find out about the Cockleshell Heroes, the Air-Sea Rescue Service, the Normandy landings, or the raft used by Pierre Boulle (author of *The Bridge on the River Kwai*) when he tried to enter Indo-China as a secret agent. You should have no difficulty in finding books about them in your public library.

Boats in art, literature and music

6

Artists find boats a never-ending source of interest. You may like to think of reasons for this. Look at the graceful curves in the shape of a boat and the patterns masts and sails make against the sky, or notice the dramatic effect of waves curling under the bow of a fast-moving boat or breaking over the deck in a storm. Look at pictures as though you are a detective and see what you can tell from them about the weather, the time of day, or the tide, as well as what kinds of boat the artist has seen and whether they are modern or not.

Old pictures will show you how boats used to be built in heavy wood, with heavy oars or sails. Compare these with boats in modern pictures.

'A view of Deventer' by the Dutch painter van Ruysdael, born c. 1600, died 1670. National Gallery, London. What does the sky tell you about the weather?

'Venice : a regatta on the Grand Canal' by Canaletto, 1697–1768. National Gallery, London. Contrast the decorated boats for spectators with the racing boats. Canaletto painted more than one regatta like this. Can you find another and compare them?

If you look at pictures of big ships you will often find that the artist has filled the water round the main vessel with many small boats. For what purposes are they being used? Look, too, and see how accurate the artist has been in drawing his boats. Some artists are very careful about detail and others are 'impressionistic' – they give you an outline of the boat and leave you to imagine you can see detail that is not actually there.

If you visit a seaside or riverside town, look out for its local art gallery or museum. Sometimes quite small galleries have excellent collections of local pictures. Of course, the bigger city galleries have paintings by famous artists. See if you can identify boating pictures by Canaletto and Turner, for example. Rubens, the Flemish painter, Cuyp, the seventeenth-century Dutch artist, Monet, a Frenchman, and Constable from England, all painted boats. Compare their pictures and others you find. Think about which you like best and why you prefer one to another.

Each artist has his own distinctive style, so if two great artists paint a similar scene the pictures they produce will be quite

different. Look closely and see if you can work out what makes
the style so personal to the artist. You will find it easier to
recognise an artist's style if you can see several of his pictures.
Canaletto painted a number of pictures of Venetian canals,
which you can compare.

If you cannot easily visit art galleries your library may be able
to help with illustrated art books. These will also show you
pictures which belong to galleries in other countries or which
are in privately owned collections.

You will find boating pictures in many places besides art
galleries. Watch out for travel posters, calendars, postcards,
newspapers and magazines, and inn signs.

Boats are sometimes shown on postage stamps. Look through
your own or your friends' collections, or consult a stamp
catalogue. Countries most likely to use boats for stamp designs
are islands or countries with a coastline. Some examples are
Aden, Fiji, France, the USA, and Britain.

'The Miraculous
Draught of Fishes' *by
Rubens, 1577–1640.
National Gallery,
London. This is a very
different style from
Canaletto's or van
Ruysdael's.*

Boats in literature

Where there are boats there is adventure or danger, fun or holidays, so it is not surprising that writers make full use of them. Arthur Ransome wrote a well-known series of boating stories involving the Walker family, of which *Swallows and Amazons* is the first. You may have seen the film which was made from this book. These books are full of detail about handling small boats. In *We Didn't Mean to Go to Sea* the Walker children find themselves adrift off Harwich in a fog and later sail across the North Sea to Holland in a gale.

Another adventure story in which boats play a big part is *Treasure Island* by Robert Louis Stevenson. See what you can find out about Ben Gunn's coracle in the story and what Jim Hawkins did with it.

You may enjoy reading *Three Men in a Boat* by Jerome K. Jerome. This story is about three rather accident-prone young men who take a boating holiday on the Thames. Published in 1889, this is still thought to be one of the funniest novels ever written. Whether you agree or not will depend on your own sense of humour. Here is an example from the book:

> Of all experiences in connection with towing, the most exciting is being towed by girls. It is a sensation that nobody ought to miss. It takes three girls to tow always; two hold the rope, and the other one runs round and round and giggles . . . . They get the line round their legs, and have to sit down on the path and undo each other. . . .
> They fix it straight, however, at last, and start off at a run
> . . . . At the end of a hundred yards they are naturally breathless, and suddenly stop, and all sit down on the grass and laugh, and your boat drifts out to mid-stream and turns round, before you know what has happened, or can get hold of a scull.
> Then they stand up, and are surprised.
> 'Oh, look!' they say; 'He's gone right out into the middle.'

Do you agree with the young men or are you on the girls' side?

Another story you could follow up for its boating interest is *The Wind in the Willows* by Kenneth Grahame.

Boats are mentioned several times in the Bible. Look in the Old Testament at the story of Noah's Ark (Genesis, Chapters 6–8) and retell it with drawings of your own. An early example of a coracle-type boat was the little vessel in which Moses was hidden in the bulrushes (Exodus, Chapter 2). In the New Testament see if you can find the references to boats and fishing in the gospels according to St Matthew, St Mark and St Luke.

If you like poetry look out for 'Sea Fever' by John Masefield. This poem, which begins 'I must go down to the seas again, to the lonely sea and the sky', tells of the magnetic attraction sailing has for the poet. Read the poem aloud and see if you can hear the choppy, tossing rhythms of the sea.

A *Child's Garden of Verses* by Robert Louis Stevenson contains several poems in which a small boy invents make-pretend boats to take him on imaginary voyages.

'Girls in a boat on a lotus-pond'. *No. 37 from The Hundred Poems Explained by the Nurse, by Hokusai, 1760–1849.*

Boats in music

'The Eton Boating Song' was written to encourage team spirit and school loyalty in the boys of Eton College. It begins 'Jolly boating weather/And a hay harvest breeze,/Blade on the feather,/Shade off the trees . . .' Can you find out about the rowing technique of 'Blade on the feather'? See if you can find the music and recognise the rowing rhythm in it.

Another tune you can learn is the 'Song of the Volga Boatmen'. This is a Russian folk song. Look on the map and see where the river Volga is. This music also has a strong and regular rhythm to help the crew keep in time with each other in their work.

A song connected with fishing is 'Caller Herrin'' (fresh herring) This comes from Scotland and tells of the dangers and hardships the fishermen suffer to bring the fish to the market. You should be able to find this in a collection of Scottish traditional songs and if necessary find someone to explain any difficult Scottish words.

One song with historical connections is the 'Skye Boat Song'. You probably know it already. It begins 'Speed bonny boat, like a bird on the wing/Onward, the sailors cry'. The tune and the words convey the urgency of a boat taking Bonnie Prince Charlie, 'the Young Pretender' from South Uist to Skye as he fled from Scotland at the end of his disastrous military campaign to regain the throne for the Stuarts.

If you are interested in classical music see what you can find out about Handel's 'Water Music', when it was composed and for what special purpose.

Safety, navigation, weather and rescue

7

Safety

'Rules of the road'

Tides and weather

Coastguards and rescue drill

No one wants to spoil the enjoyment of boating by always saying 'Don't', but it would be very foolish to forget the dangers of being on or in the water.

Safety

If you are sailing or canoeing you should wear a life-jacket and for white-water canoeing a special kind of crash-helmet that will let the water out. Suitable clothing is important — plimsolls, woollen pullovers (there is always a cool breeze even on a hot day) and waterproofs or 'wetsuits', like those worn by skin-divers, for colder days. If you can swim you will not panic if you fall in. Always tell someone where you are going and what time you intend to be back, so that the alarm can be raised if you are late.

If you are approaching a landing stage or another boat, keep your hands inboard (inside the gunwales) to avoid crushing your fingers. If you fall out of a rowing boat, climb back over the the stern, not over the side, to avoid flooding the boat and sinking it. If you capsize stay with the boat.

Check your equipment before setting off. You will look silly with only one oar or an empty fuel tank!

Ask about local dangers. There may be a weir, or locks, on the river. Watch a lock being operated and ask questions before you try using one yourself. Is the river tidal, or are there rocks

Treading carefully.
Note life-jackets and
sensible footwear. The
boats are firmly
secured, held steady,
with one person
moving at a time.

or shallows where you might run aground? Look and see how
busy it is. There may be tugs or barges or perhaps a ferry cutting
right across your path. Are there any low bridges where you
might have to unstep your mast? If you see notices saying 'Keep
clear', obey them! Keep an eye on the weather and on the time.

'Rules of the road'

Learn the basic rules before you launch your boat. There is no
time to look them up if you are about to collide with another
boat! Keep a proper look-out and if necessary change direction
in good time, with a positive change of course to make your
intentions clear to the other boat. Power-driven boats give way

to sailing boats, but be prepared for exceptions. For example, if you meet a large vessel which would go aground if she left the centre of the river it is up to you to move out of the way. If two boats are approaching each other head on, each should alter her own course to starboard. If you overtake another boat it is up to you to keep clear of her – do not cut across her bows. When two sailing boats approach each other the rules say that the boat with the wind coming in on the port side gives way to the boat with the wind coming in on the starboard side. If two boats have the wind on the same side the boat to windward gives way to the boat to leeward. This is because the windward boat may take too much wind from the leeward boat and put her in difficulty, especially if space is restricted.

It is useful to know about sound signals, as larger vessels may sound a siren to warn you of their movements. One short blast means they are turning to starboard. Two short blasts mean turning to port, and three mean going astern. These signals can also be given by bell.

If you are boating in a river estuary, or travelling on a cross-Channel ship, you may see buoys marking the navigable channels, or the harbour entrance. Buoys are red or red-and-white for port and black or black-and-white for starboard. They are different shapes for different purposes: can-shaped, conical, or round, and have different marks on the top of them. Study the different designs in the *Seaway Code* or any book on navigation, and draw, colour and label them. See if you can identify buoys in the water.

It is also useful to know something about the compass. This shows you where north is so that you can steer a course accurately. In a small boat you can manage with a hand-held compass if you keep it away from metal. See how much you can find out about using a compass. For example, what are the names of the points of the compass, and what is a lubberline?

Tides
The angle of buoys in the water, or of moored boats, will tell you whether the tide is flooding (coming in) or running (going

The Port Isaac inshore life-boat rescuing a yachtsman. He was right to climb on to the capsized boat, but he has no life-jacket.

out). Many small boats never go near tidal water, but if you are at the seaside or on a tidal river you need to know about tides or you may be swept out to sea. Using an inflatable dinghy at the seaside, for example, can be very dangerous. It is light and will be swept out very quickly, and you will probably not be wearing warm clothes because you were not planning to go to sea. It is safest not to use a small boat when the tide is going out. Even a motor boat's engine may fail and leave you drifting helplessly, so it is wise not to take the risk.

If you are on a larger sea-going yacht or motor launch with an experienced skipper you can of course use the tide to speed your journey. This is why fishermen will set out in the middle of the night if the tide is right.

Anchoring in tidal water is also a problem, as you must allow for the water to rise and fall, floating or grounding your boat, possibly while you are ashore having your tea!

Weather

Even being caught in the middle of the park boating lake in a heavy rain shower can be uncomfortable, so it is sensible to go boating only when the weather looks suitable. If you are rowing, or in a motor boat, you will not want the water to be too rough. If you are sailing it is best if the wind is steady and not blowing in strong and sudden gusts.

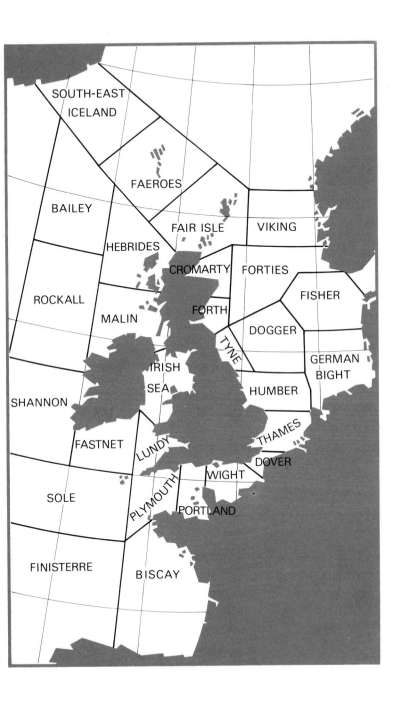

Coastal sea areas referred to in weather forecasts.

Listen to weather forecasts from national and local radio stations. Forecasts for inshore waters (up to 19·3 km (12 miles) from the coast) are useful even for rivers as they can help you guess what weather is coming inland from the sea. These forecasts are usually late at night (23.45 hours in England — 23.20 in Scotland on BBC Radio 4) but perhaps you could arrange for someone to tape record one for you. The forecasts tell you about visibility, wind, barometric pressure, and so on. See if you can find out more about these.

You may have heard people refer to wind force. This is measured on the Beaufort Wind Scale which ranges from 0 (calm, wind less than 1·6 kph (1 mph)) to 12 (hurricane, wind over 120 kph (75 mph)). Consult the *Seaway Code* or another navigation book for the complete list. You might like to keep a weather diary for a week or two, noting signs such as how much the wind moves tree branches, or makes flags flutter, or blows leaves or paper about, or makes walking hard work. Estimate the wind force from these clues. If you can listen to weather forecasts in the same weeks you can check your guesses.

At sailing clubs you may see flags flying showing whether or not sailing is allowed that day. This depends on the club officials' judgment of whether or not the wind force is too high for safety. In a high wind you may see conical shapes hoisted in harbours or at Coastguard stations. These are gale warnings. A North Cone (one with a point at the top) means a gale from the north. A South Cone (with the point at the bottom) means a gale from the south. No small boat should be out in a gale, which means the wind is Force 7 or more.

Clouds will also tell you what weather is coming. *Cumulus* looks like small pieces of cotton wool and means good weather. If the small clouds join up to make bigger ones, though, change is on the way. See what you can find out about *nimbus, stratus* and *cirrus* clouds. Add your observations about clouds to your weather diary. Make your observations at the same times each day, for example when you reach your classroom in the morning, at lunchtime, and when you arrive home. Then you can see if there is a weather pattern.

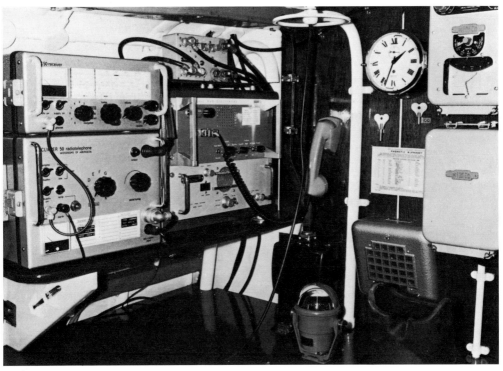

Inside a Solent class 14·6 m (48 ft) life-boat.

Coastguards and rescue drill

Coastguard stations co-ordinate rescue services around the coast. They run a scheme called CG66 by which they keep a record of boats which use a particular stretch of water regularly, and also of boats whose owners tell them they are travelling from one point to another. Then if a boat is overdue they can begin a search. If you tell the coastguards about a planned journey you must remember to report your safe arrival to them.

If you are in serious difficulty, or if you find someone else in difficulty, you will need to know what signs to make or what signs they are making to you. The Morse Code for the distress signal 'SOS' (Save Our Souls) is three dots, three dashes and three dots. The 'SOS' can be made by light, sound or any available means. The other distress call you may come across is MAYDAY (a shorthand developed from the French for 'help me' — aidez-moi, which became m'aidez, then mayday). Other distress signals are: a red flare or rocket, an orange smoke flare, flames from something burning such as a rag soaked in oil, clothing waved on an oar, someone raising and lowering outstretched arms, a continuous sound on a whistle or siren, or a flag flying upside down or with anything round-shaped above or below it. If you are on shore and see or hear any of these out to sea, contact the local coastguard or police at once by dialling 999 at the nearest telephone.

Australian surf-boat used for rescue work. The strong, fit crew are greatly respected for their skill.

Useful addresses and books

8

Organisations

Places of interest

Books

Organisations

British Canoe Union. The Secretary, 70 Brompton Road, London, SW3 1DT.

British Waterways Board. Enquiry Office, British Waterways Board, Melbury House, Melbury Terrace, London, NW1 6JX. For information about waterways controlled by the Board. Their *Address Book* contains details of clubs, societies, and organisations concerned with waterways.

Highlands and Islands Development Board, Bridge House, 27 Bank Street, Inverness, IV1 1QR. 'Yachting and Boating' leaflet contains information about sailing schools, canoe instruction, boat clubs, etc., in N. W. Scotland.

Hover Club of Great Britain. The Secretary, 128 Queens Road, Portsmouth, Hants, PO2 7NE, to whom enquiries about the Schools National Hovercraft Competition should be addressed.

Inland Waterways Association, 114 Regent's Park Road, London, NW1 8UQ.

London Motor Boat Racing Club. The Secretary, 90 Ferrymead Avenue, Greenford, Middlesex. Races are held at Woodlands Lake, Iver Heath, Bucks (on the A4007 road) on a number of Saturday afternoons March–October (fixture list from the Secretary).

Longridge Scout Boating Centre. The Warden, Longridge Scout Boating Centre, Quarry Wood Road, Marlow, Bucks. The National Scout Association Boating Centre.

Royal National Life-boat Institution. Head Office, RNLI, West Quay Road, Poole, Dorset, BH15 LHZ.

Royal Yachting Association. Victoria Way, Woking, Surrey. For information about racing (including powerboat racing).

Strathclyde Police, Glasgow. Police offices throughout Glasgow have a Community Involvement Officer who will answer questions.

Places of interest

Arbuthnot Museum, Peterhead, Aberdeenshire. Collection of fishing boats.

Bayle Museum, Bridlington, Yorks. Display of model boats.

Beecroft Art Gallery, Westcliff, Southend-on-Sea, Essex. Pictures of the Thames Estuary.

Bridewell Museum, Norwich. Boat-building and fishing equipment.

British Museum, Great Russell Street, London, WC1. See Nineveh and Egyptian galleries.

Exeter Maritime Museum. International collection well worth visiting. Enquiries to the Director, International Sailing Craft Association, The Quay, Exeter. School parties welcome.

Museum and Art Gallery, Bridport, Dorset. Display of fishing nets, etc.

National Maritime Museum, Greenwich. The Education Officer will answer questions on specific points, and special talks can be arranged for school parties. Sir Francis Chichester's *Gypsy Moth IV* is on view nearby in Greenwich.

North Western Museum of Inland Navigation. New museum being established at Ellesmere Port. Enquiries to Dr David Owen, The Museum, Manchester University, M13 9PL.

Science Museum, South Kensington, London, SW7. Display of boats.

Scottish Fisheries Museum, St Ayles, Harbourhead, Anstruther, Fife. Fishing gear.

South Shields Museum, South Shields, Co. Durham. Model life-boats.

South Yorkshire Industrial Museum, Cusworth Hall, Doncaster, DN5 7TU. Contains a canal room.

Southwold Museum, Southwold, Suffolk. Model boats, fishing nets.

Southwold Sailors' Reading Room, Southwold, Suffolk. Local boating relics and photographs.

Tate Gallery, Millbank, London, SW1P 4RG. Many boating
  pictures.
'Thames' Division Museum (Metropolitan Police). The Curator,
  'Thames' Division Police Station, 98 Wapping High Street,
  London, E1. Open to organised parties over the age of 12,
  on written request, when police work permits.
Waterways Museum, Stoke Bruerne, near Towcester, Northants,
  NN12 7SE.

Books

Blandford, Percy, *An illustrated history of small boats,* Spurbooks,
  1974.
Boulle, Pierre, *The source of the river Kwai,* Secker & Warburg,
  1967.
Burgess, F. H., *A dictionary for yachtsmen,* David & Charles,
  1974.
Caunter, J. A. L., *Shark angling in Great Britain*, Allen & Unwin,
  1961.
Colver, Hugh, *This is the hovercraft,* Hamish Hamilton, 1972.
Davies, John, *Sailing,* Hamlyn, paperback, 1972.
Hadfield, Charles, *Introducing inland waterways,* David &
  Charles, 1973.
Hankinson, John, *Canal cruising,* Ward Lock, 1967.
Howarth, Patrick, *The Life-boat story,* Routledge & Kegan Paul,
  1957.
Hubbard, Donald, *Ships-in-bottles,* David & Charles, 1971.
Irving, J., *Knots, ties and splices,* Routledge & Kegan Paul,
  revised edition 1976.
Lindley, Kenneth, *Seaside and seacoast,* Routledge & Kegan
  Paul (Local Search Series), 1975.
McLeavy, Roy (ed.), *Jane's surface skimmers, hovercraft and
  hydrofoils,* Jane's Yearbooks, annually.
Middleton, E. W., *Discovering life-boats,* Shire Publications,
  paperback, 3rd revised edition, 1974.
Mudie, Colin, *Motor boats and boating,* Hamlyn, paperback,
  1972.
Nicholl, G. W. R., *Inflatable boats,* Adlard Coles, 1969.
Purton, Rowland W., *Rivers and canals,* Routledge & Kegan

Paul (Local Search Series), 1972.

Seaway Code, a guide for small boat users, HMSO for the Department of Trade and Industry and the Central Office of Information, paperback, 1974.

Sutherland, Charles, *Modern canoeing,* Faber, 1964.

Acknowledgments

Author and publishers wish to thank the following for permission to reproduce illustrations on the pages listed : Australian Information Service, Australian High Commission, London, pp. ii–iii, 4, 15 (photos J. Fitzpatrick), p. 8(i) (Australian News and Information Bureau, photo Neil Murray), and p. 28 (AOP) ; Avon Inflatables Ltd, pp. 13, 30; Blakes (Norfolk Broads Holidays) Ltd, pp. 2, 27, 60 (photos Fuller's) ; the Trustees of the British Museum, pp. 45, 57 ; British Rail, pp. 6, 38 ; British Waterways Board, pp. 5, 14, 31, 42(i) (photos D. Pratt) ; Burgee Marine Ltd, p. 18 ; Exeter Maritime Museum, pp. 10, 46, 66 ; the Fijian Government, p. 9 ; H.M. Customs & Excise, p. 37 ; *Midlands Power*, p. 26 ; the Trustees, the National Gallery, London, pp. 53, 54, 55 ; the National Maritime Museum, London, pp. 8(ii), 47, 48 ; P & O, p. 39 ; E. Rogers, pp. 50, 51 ; Royal National Life-boat Institution, pp. 3, 40, 62, 65 ; Spurbooks Ltd (from P. Blandford, *An illustrated history of small boats*) pp. 12, 23, 25 ; Tyne Canoes Ltd, p. 22.

The local search series

Editor: Mrs Molly Harrison MBE, FRSA

This book is one of a highly successful series designed to help young people to look inquiringly and critically at particular aspects of the world about them. It encourages them to think for themselves, to seek first-hand information from other people, to make the most of visits to interesting places, and to record their discoveries and their experiences.

Many boys and girls enjoy detective work of this kind and find it fun to look for evidence and to illustrate their findings in ways that appeal to them. Such lively activities are equally rewarding whether carried out individually or in a group.